Who Needs a PRAIRIE?

A Grassland Ecosystem

KAREN PATKAU

TUNDRA BOOKS

Published in Canada by Tundra Books, a division of Random House of Canada, One Toronto Street, Suite 300, Toronto, Ontario M5C 2V6

Published in the United States by Tundra Books of Northern New York, P.O. Box 1030, Plattsburgh, New York 12901

Library of Congress Control Number: 2013943891

Library and Archives Canada Cataloguing in Publication

Patkau, Karen, author
        Who needs a prairie? : a grassland ecosystem / Karen Patkau.

(Ecosystem series)
Ages 7-10.
Issued in print and electronic formats.
ISBN 978-1-77049-388-9 (bound) – ISBN 978-1-77049-389-6 (epub)

        1. Grassland ecology – Juvenile literature. I. Title. II. Series: Patkau, Karen. Ecosystem series.

QH541.5.P7P38 2014   j577.44   C2013-904504-X
                                                   C2013-904505-8

Edited by Sue Tate
Designed by Karen Patkau
The artwork in this book was digitally rendered.

www.tundrabooks.com

Printed and bound in China

1 2 3 4 5 6   19 18 17 16 15 14

To Dr. Jane Berg,

with special thanks to my family and friends.

WELCOME TO THE PRAIRIE

Pronghorns race over a grassy plain that rolls toward the horizon. Searching for rodents on the ground, red-tailed hawks circle in the air.

Flat-topped buttes rise above the river valley floor. A gusty wind blows clouds across the sky.

In the "badlands," scanty vegetation, rocky canyons, and sand are found. A short-horned lizard snaps up insects among sagebrush and pincushion cacti.

This wild and rugged grassland is a prairie.

LIVING ON THE PRAIRIE

The prairie is an ecosystem. Its inhabitants depend on each other and their surroundings. Let's meet more of this prairie's plants and animals.

Wheatgrass, spear grass, and blue grama are common grasses. Butterflies and bees flit among the flowers of plants called forbs. Grasshoppers leap here and there.

A yellow-bellied racer glides toward a pipit. Startled, the bird flies away. A spider spins her web, while a dung beetle rolls a dung ball across the ground.

Sage grouse and cottontail rabbits munch dandelions. Massive mother bison graze peacefully as their frisky calves romp nearby.

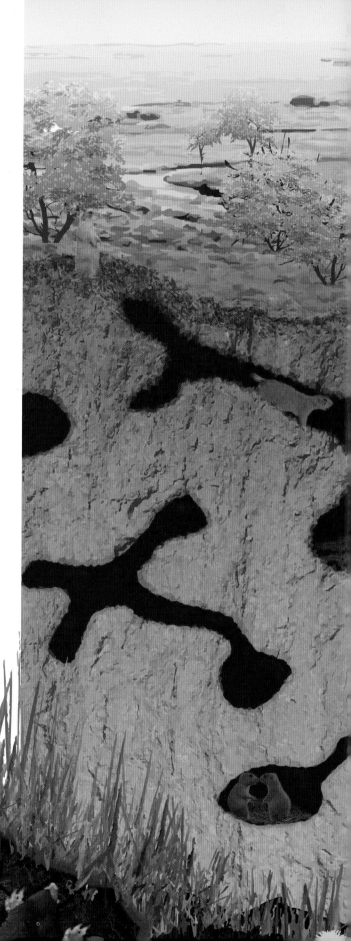

Trees and bushes line a winding creek.

In open spaces, with few tall plants for shelter, many animals live in underground burrows. Cooler in summer and warmer in winter, burrows also provide safety from predators.

Mounds of dirt mark entrances to a black-tailed "prairie dog town." In mazes of tunnels and chambers, residents take cover, sleep, raise young, and store food.

A prairie rattlesnake coils up in an empty prairie dog tunnel. Burrowing owls move into another one. They line theirs with feathers and leaves.

Moles, earthworms, and ants dig their way through the soil and tangled roots. They loosen up the earth, making room for air and water to pass through.

PRAIRIE SEASONS

The prairie has four distinct seasons. Weather conditions can be extreme.

Prairie crocuses signal spring. Fresh green grass sprouts around a slough – a rain-filled prairie pothole. Twin mule deer fawns stand on wobbly legs.

In summer, long-billed curlews nest in the grasses. A swift fox suns near his den. Vetches, buttercups, and other flowers blossom.

Summer heat can bring strong winds, thunderstorms, wildfires, and drought.

In autumn, the prairie turns golden. Ripe seeds are scattered by the wind and by the movements and droppings of birds and animals.

Cool, crisp days become shorter. Frosty nights get longer. Some creatures travel to warmer lands. For those remaining, it is the last chance to eat well for months.

When winter cold arrives, skies may be clear or blizzards may blow across the grassland. Plants lie dormant beneath the snow. Animals forage as best they can.

THE FOOD CHAIN

To stay alive, all living things need food.
When one living thing eats another and,
in turn, is eaten by something else, a food
chain forms.

Plants make their own food, using water,
carbon dioxide from the air, and energy
from the sun.

Animals eat other living things. A
herbivore is a plant-eater, like the vole,
which eats plants and seeds.

The badger eats both plants and animals.
It is an omnivore. A carnivore is a meat-
eater, like the black-footed ferret.

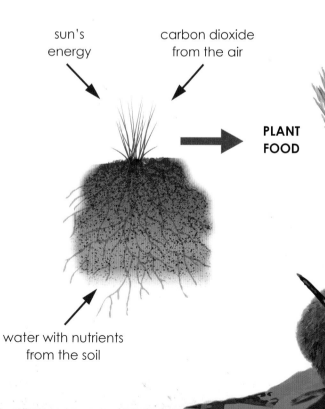

sun's
energy

carbon dioxide
from the air

PLANT
FOOD

water with nutrients
from the soil

BACTERIA

LIFE IS A CYCLE

For all living things, life eventually ends. Scavengers eat the remains of plants and dead animals.

Coyotes prefer fresh meat, but will also eat rotting meat.

Some bacteria and fungi are decomposers. They live on dead matter and break it down, releasing nutrients back into the environment. Plants need nutrients to grow.

Mushrooms are a type of fungus. Their caps and stems sprout above ground, while their white threadlike fibers, called hyphae, spread out below.

FIRE RESTORES THE LAND

Near the end of summer, the prairie looks dry and lifeless. Dark clouds loom above the horizon in the late afternoon. Lightning zigzags and flashes. Thunder cracks and booms. Rain pours down. The parched earth soaks up the rainwater.

After the storm, a meadowlark sings, "*To-to-toleeoo-to-to, to-to-toleeoo-to-to.*" A rainbow arches across the vast sky.

A withered bush has been struck by lightning. It smolders and sparks.

Soon, windblown flames race across the land. Creatures disappear into burrows or flee to safety.

Trees, shrubs, and grasses burn. Underground, the strong grass roots survive.

Finally, the fire dies down. Some large plants have been destroyed. Now there is more light, room, and soil for grasses and other native plants.

This fire has helped restore the prairie.

THE GREAT PLAINS

In the middle of North America is an immense stretch of grassland. This patchwork of natural and farmed land is called the Great Plains.

For thousands of years, only Native North Americans lived here. Enormous herds of bison and pronghorn roamed. Like waves in the sea, wild grasses swayed in the wind.

Within the last two centuries, settlers displaced native plants and animals with farms and ranches. Native people were moved to reserves.

Settlers planted crops on moist eastern soil, where tall and midsized grasses grew. Dry western land, with its short grasses, became pastureland for cattle and sheep.

PRAIRIE PLANTS PROTECT THE LAND

Prairie plants suit their environment. Their far-reaching roots dig into the ground to anchor them and find water.

Soil, matted with grass and roots, forms a dense layer called sod, which protects the roots from freezing in winter and burning in fire.

When farmers plow sod to plant crops, nutrient-rich topsoil can erode – be blown away by wind or washed away by rain.

Unlike most plants, which sprout from their tips, grass develops from its base. If grass is eaten or burned away, new blades soon shoot up.

However, if large numbers of ranch animals eat grass faster than new blades can grow, its roots will die. Land then becomes dry and barren.

SOD

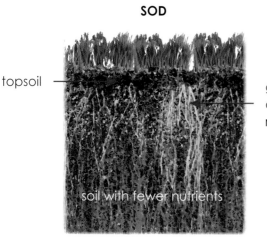

topsoil

grass and roots

soil with fewer nutrients

WHO NEEDS A PRAIRIE?

Earth's temperature is rising, partly because of human activities. When we burn fuel to create electricity or run machines, it produces heat-trapping greenhouse gases.

This global warming changes the amounts of snow and rain that fall in different places. Where grassland gets wetter, forests grow. Where it gets drier, deserts form.

Earth's population and its need for food is increasing. Much of the world's food is grown on grassland.

Wheat, oats, rye, barley, and corn are crops that thrive on the prairie. We use them in flour, cereal, cooking oil, and animal feed.

When we plant crops and spray them with insect-killing chemicals, it becomes hard for prairie wildlife to survive.

In spite of a few protected and restored areas, very little "natural" grassland remains today.

Who needs a prairie? We all do.

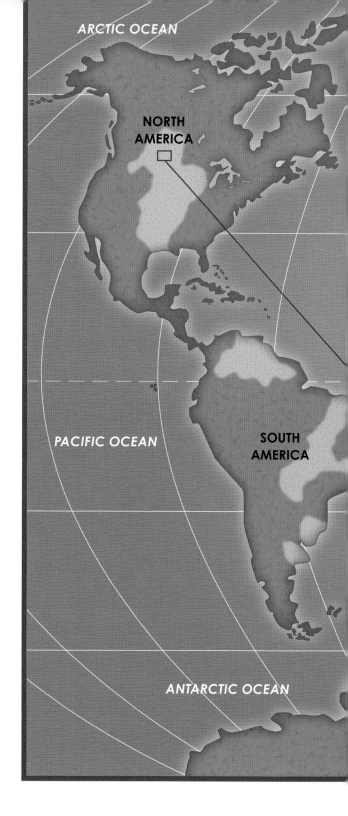

GRASSLAND AREAS OF THE WORLD

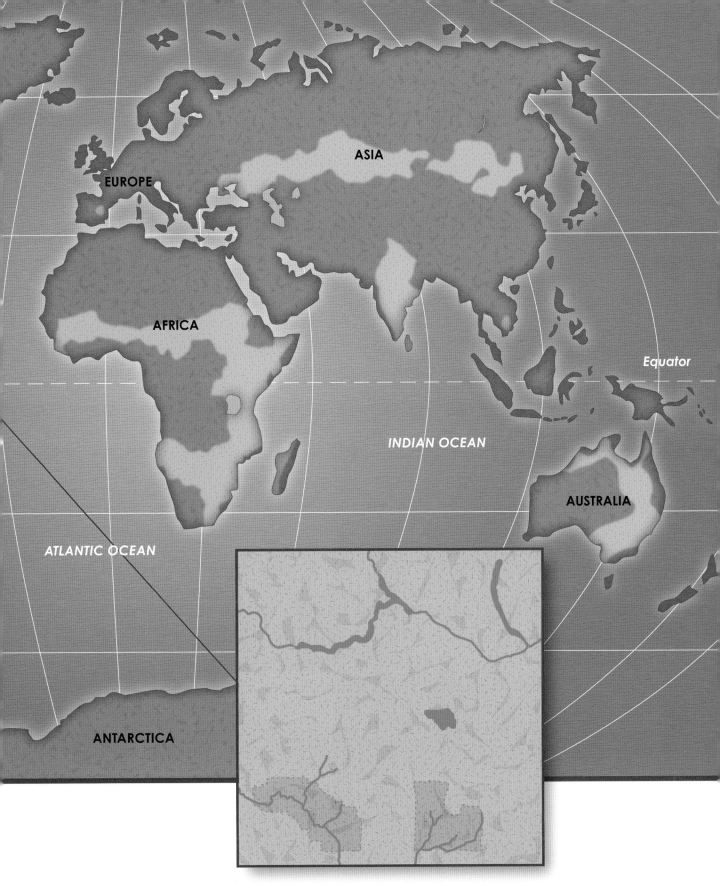

The prairie described in this book is in central North America.

HERE IS MORE INFORMATION ABOUT SOME OF THE PRAIRIE INHABITANTS:

Badger
The badger is a fierce, strong animal. An excellent digger, it sometimes hunts with a fast-moving coyote. They help each other find, chase, and trap burrowing prey.

Bison
The bison is the largest land animal in North America. A herbivore, it eats mostly grass. By rolling in dirt, it rids itself of its heavy winter coat and insect pests.

Black-Footed Ferret
This ferret is very rare in the wild. Nocturnal, it is active at night and hunts sleeping prairie dogs. The "prairie bandit" likes to live in abandoned prairie dog burrows.

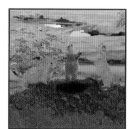

Black-Tailed Prairie Dogs
These members of the squirrel family are playful and sociable. They communicate by mixing different sounds and actions. Prairie dogs do not hibernate in winter.

Burrowing Owl
When threatened, this tiny ground-dwelling owl mimics the rattling hiss of a rattlesnake. It hunts both day and night for insects, birds, snakes, frogs, and mice.

Buttercups
Poisonous, fresh buttercups have a bitter taste and cause blisters in the mouth and stomach. When dried, they have less poison. Hay containing buttercups is safe for animals to eat.

Dung Beetle
The dung beetle rolls small lumps of animal dung, particularly herbivore waste, back to its burrow. It eats and buries the dung, recycling nutrients into the soil.

Forbs
Along with grasses, many of these nonwoody or herbaceous plants are found on the prairie. Their brightly colored blossoms are commonly known as wildflowers.

Grasses
Although their flowers have no petals, grasses are the largest family of flowering plants. On the hot dry prairie, little moisture is lost from their long, thin leaves.

Grasshopper
This plant-eating insect can jump, walk, and fly. It uses antennae on its head to smell and feel. It breathes through holes along the sides of its body called spiracles.

Long-Billed Curlew
In the warm muddy lands where it spends the winter, this large shorebird uses its long curved bill to capture shrimp and crabs. In summer prairie pastures, it digs up earthworms.

Mole
A small furry animal with a hairless snout, the mole has powerful front claws for digging underground. Its eyes are tiny and it does not see well.

Pincushion Cactus

This ball-shaped plant is covered in sharp spines and topped with bright flowers. Its fleshy stem soaks up and stores water. After blooming, it sprouts sweet berries.

Pipit

Flying high in the sky, this prairie songbird sings a high-pitched tune, "*Tzee-tzee-tzee-tzee-tzee.*" On the ground, it eats insects, spiders, and seeds.

Prairie Crocuses

Crocus plants are covered in fuzzy white hairs. Their gray-green leaves do not appear until their blue or purple flowers fade. Crocuses grow better after a wildfire.

Pronghorns

Pronghorns are the fastest land animals in North America. They are named for the branched, pointed horns on the male's head. The female's horns are smaller and straight.

Red-Tailed Hawks

These birds of prey have keen eyesight and can spot a tiny mouse from high above. Their shrill, raspy cries pierce the air. Red-tailed hawks usually mate for life.

Sagebrush

This hardy silver-gray bush is fragrant, especially when wet. Its yellow flowers bloom in late summer and early fall. Sage grouse and pronghorns eat sagebrush.

Sage Grouse

In early spring, male sage grouse form groups and strut about to attract females. Sage grouse like to nest under the protective cover of sagebrush.

Short-Horned Lizard

This small, squat lizard has a fringe of pointed scales around its head and sides. Diurnal, it is active during the day. At night, it burrows into the ground.

Swift Fox

The nocturnal, cat-sized fox hunts insects and small animals. Coyotes, badgers, and eagles prey on it. This little fox dislikes being out in the wind.

Vetch

An annual plant, the vetch sprouts, flowers, and dies within a year. Part of the legume or pea family, the vetch bears fruit in the form of a pod containing up to twelve seeds.

Vole

Similar to a mouse, the vole has a stockier body and a shorter tail. Like all rodents, its large, sharp-edged front teeth continue to grow as chewing wears them down.

Yellow-Bellied Racer

A hunter during the day, this long slender snake with excellent vision is built for speed. It hibernates during the winter, either alone or with other snakes, in a den.

GLOSSARY

bacteria – tiny single-celled organisms that break down the remains of other living things

buttes – hills with steep sides and flat tops that rise abruptly from flat land

decomposers – organisms that break down dead matter, such as bacteria, fungi, and some types of worms

dormant – an inactive state

drought – a long period of time without any rain

ecosystem – a community of plants, animals, and organisms that interact with each other and their physical environment. There are many different ecosystems on Earth.

environment – the surroundings and conditions in which something exists or lives

forage – to wander in search of something, especially food

fungi – nongreen plants, such as mushrooms and molds, which live off other things

global warming – the rise in average temperature of air near the earth's surface since the mid-twentieth century

grassland – land covered mainly by grasses and nonwoody plants. There are two main types of grassland. Prairies occur in cool, dry areas of the world. Savannas occur in warm or hot climates, with more rain.

greenhouse gases – gases in the earth's atmosphere that trap heat. The main greenhouse gases are carbon dioxide, methane, and nitrous oxide.

hibernate – to spend the winter in an inactive sleeplike state

inhabitants – living things that dwell in a certain place for a period of time

nutrients – substances that give nourishment to a living thing

nutrition – the process of providing substances necessary for health and growth

predators – animals that hunt other animals for food

prey – an animal that is hunted by another animal for food

topsoil – the upper layer of soil that supplies plants with nourishment

vegetation – plant life in a particular place or ecosystem